General and Social
Letter Writing

GENERAL AND SOCIAL LETTER WRITING

By
A. G. ELLIOT

Author of Business Letters, Contracts and Etiquette;
Non-fiction Writing and Publishing; Publisher of
Right Way Books, etc.

PAPERFRONTS
ELLIOT RIGHT WAY BOOKS
KINGSWOOD SURREY U.K.

Printed in Great Britain by
Cox & Wyman Ltd., London, Reading and Fakenham

Introduction

The Purpose of a Letter

LETTERS are written for all sorts of purposes and in many instances are comparatively easy. In this book I propose largely to confine myself to giving samples of *simple* requirements in correspondence, such as the answer to an invitation or a letter of sympathy. When we come to the more difficult letter I shall try to go into the basic principles, which should enable the reader to tackle these more effectively.

It may be some consolation to those who find difficulty to know that even the experienced writer is often confronted with a problem and, like the beginner, finds himself staring at paper without a thought or a word to put on it. It is useless to sit and look at the paper for a long time, because the mind is apt to become over concentrated on its task; far better to drop the matter for a few hours or even a day or two and come back to it again, when ideas may flow more readily.

I also hope that in studying the relevant passages in this book you will find that the ideas required are stimulated.

Contents

8 CONTENTS

1

Outline of requirements

Paper

THE quality, thickness, size and colour to be used are mainly individual matters depending upon taste and purse. Very thin or flimsy paper should be avoided as it looks cheap and unless one uses a typewriter the size is immaterial, although too small a sheet is wasteful on account of the margins. Lined paper although used by many does not make the finished letter so attractive and it is therefore wiser to use a plain sheet.

For those writing to friends abroad it is, of course, essential to use thin material as airmail rates are so expensive. Where possible the airmail letter form is the cheapest way with overseas mail.

White paper is of course correct, but tinted papers and pale blues are very fashionable. I always think it is better to avoid such colours as pale pink and yellow but here again it is largely a matter of taste. Bright colours are apt to look flamboyant, although quite often used by business concerns as a form of advertisement. However, they are better avoided in social letters.

Writing Materials

It should hardly be necessary to say that writing or addressing an envelope in pencil is not considered good taste, but some people still do it. There is always the possibility, when writing in pencil that it might become rubbed out or faded, particularly in the rather damp English climate. Always use ink unless there is some special reason, for example where one happens to be without a pen; but apologize in the letter for using the pencil. It could even be regarded as rather an insult to the recipient should an apology not be made. The ball-point is the kind of pen most commonly in use today, but there are many people who prefer the "cleaner" look of a letter written with a fountain-pen.

This leaves the choice between ink and type-writer. The typewriter is, of course, advisable for all business correspondence owing to the clarity and speed with which the letter can be read, but many people consider it bad form to use a typewriter for personal or social letters and there is no question that the typed letter is less friendly and intimate than the handwritten one. For long social letters or where handwriting is difficult to read, however, provided in the letter one inserts an excuse or apology for using a typewriter, it is all right to do so.

In the course of my work I receive many hundreds of letters and they are written in various coloured inks, although mostly in the common blue-black. Here again it is considered better taste to use a blue ink than some fancy heliotrope or brown, although some people might consider this view to be old-fashioned and prefer to have some colour on their paper. Indeed, owing to their professional requirements, a great many chartered accountants, printers and authors use special tinted inks for their work and also use them in their private letters.

All letters should be hand signed, but where one's signature is illegible this can be typed or written in block capitals in addition to the hand-written signature, the latter being essential.

Handwriting

The purpose of handwriting is to be read easily. It is an insult to your friends to write in a hand which causes difficulty in reading, because it occupies their time unnecessarily. Hardly a day passes but I have to hand a letter to one or other of my staff to see if they can decipher a word and in some instances letters are so badly written that they have to be typed before I can answer them.

I do, therefore, appeal to all those who are perhaps under the mistaken impression that their writing shows great character to forget about the character and try and write clearly.

"Good" handwriting is small and neat but not too small to be read. Avoid flourishes, loops, whirls and curly letters, unless you have "copper-plate" style, for unless they are part of formed handwriting they are easily detected as flamboyant appendages.

Envelopes

It is, of course, nice when a tinted paper is used with an envelope to match. For the social letter most people prefer the rather square envelope to the more oblong one which is used for general business purposes, but there is really no rule and any size or colour of envelope can be used as its only purpose is safely to convey the contents through the post. Some people might consider it *infra dig* to use the cheap manilla envelope for a private letter and, of course, it would be quite out of place to use such a cheap envelope for an invitation, for example, to a wedding. It is a matter of common sense. However, it indicates good grooming to use paper and envelopes of the same colour and variety; consider the rather messy effect of a blue envelope and white paper, especially when they do not fit.

An important point which many people do not realize is that the entire name and address should be written in the lower half of the envelope. To write it partly in the upper half means that although the writing may not be covered by the stamp or stamps, it frequently is by a heavy black postmark. Write envelopes very carefully, always making sure, as far as possible, that the full address is written. The Post Office prefer that the Postal

Wrong: Address too high, stamp too low

Miss Jean Wilson,

24 Lower Road,

CROYDON,

CR9 1FQ

Right: Address in lower half

Miss Jean Wilson,

24 Lower Road,

CROYDON,

CR9 1FQ

District (i.e. nearest town, village, etc.), is written in capitals or underlined. If you are writing to someone in your own district, write LOCAL on the bottom left-hand corner of the letter. This greatly helps the Sorting Office.

The British Post Office has begun to introduce a new computerised sorting system which requires the use of postal codes. The British system is based on *number and letter* codes (e.g. RH1 5RG). These are difficult for the Postmen to distinguish unless they are written very clearly in capitals.

Other countries, such as the U.S.A. and Australia have numerical 'zip' codes (digits only) which seems to me to be much more sensible. Whatever one's personal opinion may be, however, it is important to include the code as the last line of the address on the front of the envelope, and to put your own post code on your own letter heading.

When your letter arrives at the Post Office, an operator will type the postal code number on to the envelope in a special magnetic ink, and after that the letter can be sorted by an automatic machine.

In instances where you are writing to someone who may have moved from their address it is always wise to write the words "Please forward" on the top left-hand corner of the envelope; while if you are writing to someone you have not written to for a long time it is a good idea to put on the reverse of envelope (on the flap) the words "If unde-livered please return to ——" (your name and address). This helps the Post Office and saves them opening your private mail to find out to whom to return the letter. Many business houses have their name and address printed on the flap of the envelope or, where a long envelope is used on the top left-hand corner, well away from the recipient's address. Long envelopes should be addressed with the flap on the left.

Poste Restante

This service is afforded to the public by the Post Office where letters can be held at any Post Office in the country until they are collected. If you should ever receive any of these take every paper of identification you have with you, for the Post Office demand them for security reasons.

Stamping

The correct place for a stamp is in the top right-hand corner of a letter. If possible use only one stamp of the right denomination, or certainly not more than two, for a row of halfpenny stamps across the top of a letter, although possibly causing great delight to children, upsets the balance of the envelope.

Registered Letters and Express Letters

Hardly anything is so annoying as to receive a registered letter containing information of little or no importance; equally it is irritating to find an express letter, when opened, contains information of no urgency. Some people seem to delight in using these methods, which cost more! The registered letter should be confined to important correspondence or enclosures. For less vital letters there is the "recorded delivery" method.

The express letter, as its name implies, is used for urgent matters and such a letter receives special attention by the Post Office at the delivery end, a messenger usually being sent with it to its destination. Various different express services exist, with different costs according to the speed.

Postcards

They seem to have gone out of fashion a good deal, although they do save an envelope and also a little time. One reason against them is that I understand the postal authorities used to deliver them more or less at their leisure. But for any brief communications of no urgency a postcard can certainly be used. Of course postcards must never be used to convey confidential information.

With a postcard the address should, of course, be on it but it is quite correct form to drop the opening "Dear Sirs" and closing "Yours faithfully" on account of space, merely signing your name.

Dating Correspondence

Quite a few people, especially those who do not write many letters, forget to insert the date. This might not matter so much if they avoided in the letter such expressions as "today week," but

all letters or postcards should be dated as a
reference.

Business Letter Headings

Many business letter headings are printed
straightforwardly in black, and are both neat and
dignified. Others particularly where the purpose is to
advertise some product, may be multi-coloured and
perhaps include pictures, art work or trade marks.

Whichever sort you choose, there are certain
requirements, some of them legal, which must be
observed.

1. The heading should show the full name of the
trader, and the full address including the county
and postal code. It should also show telex and telephone numbers.

2. In the case of a partnership or one-man business, the full style of the firm and the name of the
owner must be printed on the letter heading, and if
there is more than one partner, all the partners'
names must be given in full.

3. The requirements for a Company are more
onerous. If it is a Limited Company, the word 'Ltd.'
must appear after the name, unless the Company
holds a licence under the Companies Act allowing
them to dispense with this. Also the names of all
the Directors must be shown, again unless a special
dispensation has been granted.

Since Britain joined the Common Market, there
have also been EEC requirements to be followed.
One of these is that Companies are required to

show on Business letters, and the order forms that they make available to their customers, their place of registration, registered number, and their registered Office. The place of registration can be shown by 'registered in England' or 'registered in Scotland' as appropriate. The registered number of a Company is the one shown on its certificate of incorporation. If a business letter shows more than one address, it must indicate which one is the registered office. If only one address is shown, the fact that that is the registered office must be indicated.

These requirements apply to letter headings and order forms of the kind described above, but they do not apply to such documents as invoices or delivery notes at all.

Regarding the position of the heading, broadly speaking, the choice falls between what is called the centralized American heading where, as the name implies, the heading is in the middle of the paper, and the more British method where generally the firm's name and list of directors or partners, etc. are given on the left-hand side, while the address is on the right. But this is entirely a matter of taste and layout or appearance.

Nowadays many companies, especially the larger ones, go to a great deal of expense and trouble in producing high-quality multicolour letter-headings, often illustrating some aspect of the company's work.

The reasons for this are more for advertising than anything else, and the more old-fashioned approach, as outlined above, is sufficient for most purposes.

One of the most important matters in a letter heading is that the name of the *county* is given as well as the name of the town or village. I receive many letters from firms in small villages, such as Mayfield, which do not give the county. When replying to the letter one has to search in an A.B.C. Railway Guide or some other source of information to find the county for the address.

Whether the heading is plain or embossed is a matter of individual choice. There is no question that the embossed heading is the more attractive. However it costs more but there is no doubt that certain types of people attach considerable, if misplaced, importance to the heading being embossed. Personally, I regard it as a waste of money. There is also the method of using an embossing stamp which is a colourless raised imprint on the paper for which a stamp is cast, and is used separately on each sheet of paper. This is a cheap, easy and economical method but is generally considered to be inferior to printed and embossed paper. It is not so easily read.

The Private Letter Heading

Many of the remarks in the previous section apply here, but of course in a private letter there is actually no need to have a printed heading. When you write it yourself all you need put is your full address in the top right-hand corner or in the centre of the page. When it is in the right-hand corner the date can be inserted in the left-hand corner, or more correctly under the address. *One most important thing is to insert your telephone number, if you have one*, because here again it is annoying to have to search through telephone directories if the recipient wishes to telephone his reply. If you have a lot of correspondence and can afford it, it is, of course, nicer to have a printed letter heading. Once again the rule—be simple and adequate. Here there is no need to have your name in the heading, as this is supplied in your signature to the letter. The method of inserting your name in the heading is, however, becoming increasingly popular and probably originates from America. I think it unwise, because it prevents another member of your family from using the paper.

Below is given a suitable heading in the most usual English style.

27 Cherry Way,
Horsham,
Sussex, RH14 4BT

Horsham 69946

Note with particular care that the county "Sussex" is given and this is most important as, after all, you will not always be writing to people who are in your own locality and who know where your own village happens to be situated. An alternative type of letter heading is the centralized one, as follows:

The Green House
Tiverton Road
Swindon, SW3 4PP
Swindon 19642

The point to be noted in this heading is that the name of the house is not in inverted commas. Formerly a great many people put the name of the house in inverted commas in the belief that it was correct; modern usage does not follow this method, although it would be correct should the name of the house happen to be that of a town, for example:

"Tavistock"
Sandy Lane
Brighton, Sussex
BN2 6HH

The size of print to use is purely a matter of taste except that it should not be too small. Time and time again I have found difficulty in reading a telephone number or address, owing perhaps to poor light, on account of a very small print having been used.

These days when people are increasingly busy, many people have their name, address and telephone number printed in small print across the top of postcards. This saves a great deal of time and trouble for merely the message and the date have then to be written as well as avoiding any pitfalls that frequently occur with illegible addresses on a small card.

General Matters

In some business concerns where a great many letters are written it may be necessary to number as well as date correspondence. This is especially applicable where the firm may be writing several letters from their different departments to another concern; but for ordinary requirements, of course, there is no need to number letters.

It is most important, however, to number pages, as if this is not done clearly and the sheets become mixed it can cause delay to the recipient and is therefore inconsiderate. "Thoughtfulness for others, is the essence of good manners."

A long time ago it was considered bad form to use both sides of a sheet but in recent years it has become customary, where necessary, to do so for reasons of economy.

In social letters where folded paper is used it is considered best to begin on the first sheet, then to make page two the right-hand inside sheet, while page three becomes the left-hand inside sheet and the back page, page four. The reason for this is simply that should the letter finish within two pages it avoids writing on the back of either page and thus shows the sender's knowledge of the correct method! Below is given a diagram of the sequence of pages:

Writing order when using four page folded paper.

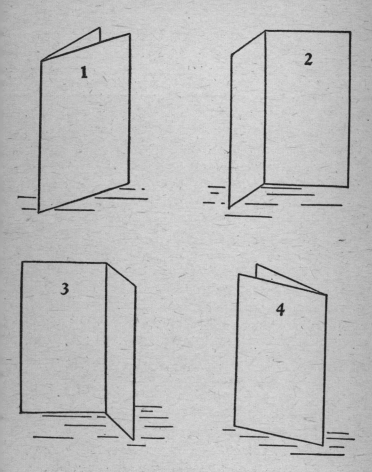

Order for using the four pages in a letter.

2
Opening and Closing

Opening

THE opening of a letter is technically known as the *Salutation*, but like Sir Winston Churchill I do not believe in using big words where small ones will do.

My correspondence shows that the opening of a letter gives more difficulty than many people realize. I am not referring to the many business letters I get from natives of West Africa who address me as "Honoured Sir" and sign themselves "Yours humbly in Jesus Christ", but to the ordinary Britisher who seems to have the greatest difficulty in knowing how to start his letter. Below I give you suitable openings for letters of many kinds.

To Parents: My dear Mother/Father (or both). Of course, this is rather formal and many people may prefer to start "My own darling Mother" or something of that nature, which is quite correct.

To Wife or Husband: My dear Joan/John. This

again is rather on the formal side and variations such as "My own one" or "My darling wife" are, of course, correct.

To Children: My dear Michael/Jennifer. Here again, especially in the case of parents writing to their children, this can be changed to "My darling . . ." Similar familiar terms can be employed in writing to any young child in the normal way. In writing to nephews or nieces the same rule would apply.

Children to Adults:
These letters are usually more informal and "My dear (or just dear) Auntie Alice" is suitable, but to a neighbour or friend "Dear Mr./Mrs. Brown."

Children to Children:
Here, of course, it is simply a case of "Dear Clive" or "Dear Mabel", unless the friendship is very close in which case the word "My" may be inserted, but it is better avoided if the child is of the opposite sex.

Adults to Adults

Old Friends and Relatives: We can hardly go wrong in using the words "My dear James" in general usage, although two girls might address each other as "Dearest". Other certain forms which it is correct to use depend upon the degree of friendship, etc. and I therefore propose to deal quite fully with this matter.

Boy and Girl Friends: Great care is necessary here as the question of feelings can arise and people are always liable to misinterpret letters which young men and girls write to each other. A young man writing to a girl asking her to play tennis or meet him somewhere would merely address her as "Dear Carol" unless the couple were friends of long standing, in which case the more intimate "My dear" might be used. But care is necessary because sometimes a girl or a man may think that if *anything other* than "Dear" is used, for example "Dearest", the writer of the letter is falling in love.

Friends and Acquaintances: The rule can be if you recall the recipient by their first name in conversation you would refer to them as "Dear Margaret", but if in talking, you address them as Mr. or Mrs. or Miss then you would use that prefix in the opening of the letter—as "Dear Mr. Jones". To clarify, very often an older man will refer to a younger man by his Christian name, but out of respect the younger refers to the older as Mr. . . . , so that in a letter he would do the same.

There is a rather subtle difference which is connected with our British class distinction: thus, two ex-public schoolboys writing to each other would probably address one another by their surnames rather than their Christian names—as "Dear Black" or "Dear Wilson"; whilst a householder writing to inquire of a jobbing gardener about his health could also say "Dear Clark"; although nowadays "Dear Mr. Clark" would be more usual.

In writing to a doctor you would generally address him as "Dear Dr. Brown", unless you were writing formally to a doctor or specialist whom you did not know, in which case the more correct form would be "Dear Sir". In writing to a clergyman if he has the letters D.D. after his name (meaning Doctor of Divinity) it would be correct to write to him as "Dr.", but if he has M.A., or has no degree, then he would be referred to as "Mr.", in the letter opening.

In writing to more than one lady at the same time, the letter should be opened thus "Ladies" or "Mesdames".

With business transactions, if the partners are male, the formal opening is "Dear Sir", or "Dear Sirs", as the case may be, or "Gentlemen" can be used, although the last is American in origin. It should be noted here that where you are writing to a director or member of a firm whom you know reasonably well you would address him as "Dear

Mr. . . .", unless you were on familiar terms where the Christian name would be used.

CLOSING

This is known as Complimentary Closing, but it means the few lines before your signature. Below are given examples.

Parents: In writing letters to a parent the correct term would be "Your affectionate son/daughter", but here individual choice has wide limits, and frequently this formal ending deteriorates into something such as "Yours lovingly", followed by your Christian name.

Cousins: Between cousins and such relatives the formal ending would be "Your affectionate cousin" or "Your loving cousin", but of course familiarity breeds contempt of formality and endings such as "Always" or "Ever" are considered suitable.

Husbands and Wives: The formal "Your affectionate husband/wife" is rarely used today and the usual closing is much less stiff, "Your own sweetheart" or "Your adoring wife/husband" and the like.

To Children: An uncle writing to his nephew or

niece could say "Your affectionate Uncle Jack" or, more simply, "Your Uncle Jack"; while any-one writing to a neighbour's child would use the more formal "Yours sincerely".

Children to Adults: The child writing to his aunt thanking her for a Christmas present could finish, "Your affectionate niece/nephew", or some less formal ending such as "With love and kisses".

Children to Children: Such a letter would be ended simply, "From Alan", except in the case of older boys and girls, who would use the more usual "Yours sincerely", or "Yours ever", unless they were on friendly terms.

Adults to Adults: In the ordinary way the clos-ing of a social letter would be "Yours sincerely" or "Yours faithfully", while a business letter would finish "Yours faithfully", "Yours truly", or "Yours very truly". Slight variations in social letters are preferred by some, such as "Sincerely yours", "Yours ever" or "Yours always", etc. The American "Your friend" or "Yours cordially" are not much favoured in this country and, of course, the ending is to some extent determined by the contents of the letter. Thus, if you are writing to somebody complain-ing that they had not paid their account, "Your friend", would be out of place and the obvious choice would be "Yours truly" or "Yours faithfully".

Boy and Girl Friends: Unless boy and girl friends have known each other for years, great care is necessary, owing to the danger of hurting feelings and the ending, "Yours sincerely", is proper. It is always wise to leave the written expressions of love for those who are engaged or getting on that way. Feelings are easily hurt. It is wise to keep on the safe side, as, in such a matter, customs differ from county to county, even from family to family. To sign oneself "Yours with love" would doubtless lead to nothing in Surrey, but in the north of Scotland it might lead to a breach of promise case!

Acquaintances and Friends: In most cases the choice simply varies between "Yours sincerely", "Yours faithfully", "Yours very truly" and "Yours truly". The first can be regarded as the more friendly, the second as more businesslike and the last two as the more formal. The old-fashioned "We remain, dear Sirs, yours truly" is rarely used except by a few people who wish to impress others or have failed to change with the times.

In writing a business letter it is usual to repeat

what you would put on the envelope, on the top of
the first page of the letter, thus:

Messrs. J. Smith & Sons,
 24, South Street,
  London, E.C.2.

Dear Sirs,

   . . . . .

or,

 John Smith, Esq.,
  24, South Street,
   London, E.C.2.

Dear Sir,

The main reason for this is so that when filing
the carbon copy it will be known under which letter
of the alphabet to file it.

In the modern rush of life, letters are becoming
less and less formal. Many of the old courtesies and
etiquettes are, perhaps sadly, vanishing. The important thing, however, is that a letter includes all
the necessary facts and information . . . all the details necessary to satisfy the recipient.

3

Punctuation and Grammar

Punctuation

THIS word "punctuation" frightens a great many people unnecessarily. Those who paid close attention at school may have no fears of punctuation, but for the rest of us it is sometimes worrying. That is the worst feature of it, namely worrying about it. Worry alone, can cause mistakes which cool judgement would discover.

The first thing to memorize is, I think, the punctuation marks, namely the comma, the semi-colon, the colon and the full stop, the question mark, the exclamation mark, inverted commas, the apostrophe, the hyphen, brackets and the dash. This seems a formidable list, but many punctuation marks are rarely used in normal letter writing.

The Comma (,)

Think always of the comma as the smallest stop; in other words put it in where in reading a sentence you would stop to breathe. Strictly speaking, a comma is unnecessary before the word "and" but it is of very little importance as long as you remember to put in your commas where a slight break in the sentence is required. If commas are left out sometimes a sentence reads wrongly and might be misunderstood. Commas are used at the end of phrases or when one would pause to take a breath, therefore, provided you do not insert one in the middle of a clause you cannot go wrong.

e.g. "Mary decided to go to London for the day the following Wednesday as she had the day off so she spent the intermediary days looking up the train fare cleaning her frock and generally working herself into a great state."

See how muddled this is, with a few commas see how different it is:

"Mary decided to go to London for the day the following Wednesday as she had the day off, so she spent the intermediary days looking up the train fare, cleaning her frock, and generally working herself into a great state."

The Semi-colon (;)

The semi-colon can be regarded as more important and is used where a slightly longer pause is required. Very often a semi-colon forms a substitute for a full stop to avoid the excessive use of new sentences, and when a contradictory phrase follows.

"Mary went to London on Wednesday, and while she was there she saw the Tower of London, and Saint Paul's Cathedral; but she did not go to

B

Westminster Abbey because she met an old friend in the Underground, who was passing through London that day.

The Colon (:)

For practical purposes the colon is employed before a list or as an indication that something is to follow, for example:

Please send the following goods:
>   1 box crackers
>   2 boxes crystallized fruits
>   6 boxes mixed nuts

The Full Stop (.)

As the name implies, this is the biggest stop of all and is used to separate sentences, as otherwise, of course, no one could make head or tail of a piece of writing. The full stop is used where a definite break is necessary and where the sentence is complete in itself. Observe the sentences in this paragraph and throughout the book.

The Exclamation Mark (!)

This is an indication of surprise, emphasis or sarcasm, as the following three examples show:

(a)   How you startled me!
(b)   Johnnie, you must do as Mummie tells you!
(c)   Fancy you thinking I wanted *that!*

The Question Mark (?)

This follows a direct question where an answer is required, but not a rhetoric question, which is merely a statement in question form. Examples of this are given below:

> (a) May I go out in the garden, please? (Direct)

> (b) "What kind of people do they think we are." (Churchill. Really a statement in question form for effect.)

Inverted Commas (" ")

People often refer to these as quotes. They are used to enclose an extract or a quotation, as for example in the words of Emerson —

"Who would be a man must be a non-conformist,"

or the doctor said —

"John will need at least six months' rest."

The Apostrophe (')

This indicates that a letter has been left out, as in changing "have not" to "haven't", it shows that the "o" has been omitted. It is also used to make a shorter and better phrase as, for example, we say "The woman's coat" rather than "The coat of the woman", but where the plural is used it must be remembered that the apostrophe goes after the "s", for instance, "The *boys'* college" and not "The *boy's* college", which would indicate that the college was for one boy!

Brackets ( )

These are used where something is put into a sentence, usually to clarify the meaning but which has no direct bearing on the sense of the sentence. Thus:

The sun was shining brightly (though not really warmly) as the clouds had now drifted apart. Alternatively, commas could be used in the place of the brackets.

Dashes and Hyphens (—)

The best explanation of a dash is to give a few examples. Often dashes are used instead of commas.

(a) I hope you are quite recovered now—we shall look forward to seeing you.
(b) How time flies—four o'clock already.
(c) Mary had to run for the train—she was late again.

The hyphen is not used so much as formerly, but certain words look better and are more clear when hyphenated. For example:

(a) Brightly-coloured flowers filled the room.

(b)   His slippers flip-flapped as he walked.

Exercise

Go back through this chapter and note where the different punctuation marks have been used and try to understand why they have been used in each instance.

Excessive punctuation, especially the use of too many exclamation marks or dashes, tends to destroy the flow of a piece of writing, so it is better to avoid excess.

GRAMMAR

The trouble with grammar, as with punctuation, is that many people tend to worry too much about it. The concentrated teaching of grammar for hours at school, in my view, has simply had the effect of making people wonder if they are writing or speaking correctly. Grammar should be learned almost unconsciously and if you listen to and read well spoken and written English you will acquire the right habit and will rarely find yourself going wrong. But there are a few rules which can be remembered as a guide.

(a)   Ask yourself what is wrong with the words "For you and I" and the answer is that it should be "For you and me". This you can prove by filling in the missing word "for", making the full phrase "For you and (for) me". You will thus see that the first phrase "For you and I" could not be correct.

(b) Always be sure that a sentence is complete; that is complete with noun and verb. Here is an example, "She went to the door to open it. But did not try." The first sentence is complete, the second is not because it has no noun. It should read "But she did not try".

Here is an example of a sentence which is incomplete because the verb has been omitted:

In the evening watching the blue sky turn slowly and imperceptibly to a warm pink. If after the words, "In the evening", are inserted the words "he was" the sentence would be complete.

(c) It is usually better not to end a sentence with a preposition. An example of this is the following sentence: But she was not the girl I wanted to go to the dance with. The sentence should read:

But she was not the girl with whom I wanted to go to the dance.

This could be further improved by cutting out the "but". "Buts" and "Ands" are words which should, as far as possible, be kept away from the beginning of sentences unless some master of the English language uses them purposely in such a position for emphasis.

(d) Another difficulty that arises is the use of "either—or" and "neither—nor". So often you read sentences such as this:
She looked, but he was neither in the lounge or in the kitchen.
Here confusion of thought has led to the mixing of the positive and negative sentence. In this—the negative sentence—it should read:
She looked, but he was neither in the lounge *nor* in the kitchen.
The positive example would be as follows:
The boy thought that his mother was either in the house or in the garden.

(e) *Split infinitive.* This is a common fault, often found in business letters. We must ask you to speedily send us your disposal instructions.
Here "speedily"—an adverb—has been inserted between the sign of the infinitive "to" and its verb "send". The sentence should read:
We must ask you speedily to send us your disposal instructions.   OR

We must ask you to send us your disposal instructions speedily.

Never separate the "to" from its verb is the rule. A good test for grammar is to read the passage aloud; if it sounds right there will not be much wrong. Use reasonable care, but don't let grammar worry you—even experts sometimes employ split infinitives for effect.

It is not the grammar that makes a letter. What matters is what it says, and what it has to say results from the amount of thought and consideration that has been given to it. The modern letter is written as if one were speaking thoughts aloud. Pack your letter with interesting news or information of value to the recipient. Worry more about the matter than about the grammar or punctuation, and you will not go far wrong.

4

Construction, Layout and Setting

MOST of us have received letters which began
at the extreme left-hand corner of the page
and filled the entire paper without any margins
and with very few paragraphs. Not only is the
effect of such a letter crowded and displeasing but
it also makes the contents difficult to understand
and follow.

The aim of letter writing is to convey information and the whole purpose of layout or construction
is to make the information easily followed by the
reader and pleasing to his eye. It is, therefore,
advisable always to leave about one inch of margin
all round the letter and sufficient space between
the lines to make them easily read. There is, however, rather more to it than that because, particularly in business letters or in social letters where
information has to be stressed, there are various
hints which can be used to this end. To give a brief
example of what I mean examine the illustrations
on page 42. Notice how striking the second letter
is by comparison with the first and how much
easier it is to see the important points. This may
seem very elementary, but the reader would be

Correct

6, Grand Road
Walsall.
Staffs.

6th Jan 1953

Dear Grace,

I have just heard that you are coming up here on the 10th of January. Do let me know if you can meet me somewhere on the 16th or 16th, naming place and time.

Looking forward to hearing from you.

Yours sincerely,
Pamela.

Incorrect

6, Grand Road,
Walsall,
Staffs,
6th January, 1953

Dear Grace,

I have just heard that you are coming up here on the 10th of January. Do let me know if you can meet me somewhere on the 15th or 16th, naming place and time.

Looking forward to hearing from you.

Yours sincerely,
Pamela

amazed if he knew the number of people who fail in matters such as these.

For instance, only today on my desk I have an answer to an inquiry for paper. In this inquiry I asked for a number of particulars such as weight, price, date of delivery, and the thickness which a book of 128 pages would make; the firm have answered everything except the last item, which they have overlooked and time must be wasted writing to them again. This is not an isolated case; similar examples occur time and time again, all involving unnecessary correspondence before the matter is rectified.

In the majority of social letters, the importance of layout is frequently negligible because most of the information conveyed is of a social character, and it is only where a date of a time of meeting or something equally essential is included that it should be set out specially clearly.

In commercial correspondence, however, it would be difficult to over-stress the importance of this setting out which makes the meaning and information so much easier to understand. To give a sample letter I will assume that I am a timber merchant quoting for whitewood battens.

Dears Sirs,
White Battens, Ravenstone Scheme

In reply to your kind inquiry, reference

172/S8, of the 28th April, 19- -, we are pleased to advise that we can supply the following:

50 × 125 mm *Battens*	
250 @ 4 metres and longer, average 4·5m.	All at £33 per M³, delivered.
50 @ 7 metres	
12 @ 8 metres	
6 @ 9 metres	

Date of Delivery

Between three and six weeks from receipt of order.

Terms

Discount of 2½% for cash within 7 days. Alternatively, monthly account, net.

The stock offered is best quality Finnish white and we hope to receive your valued order.

Yours faithfully,

Comments on the Above Letter

By making the heading clear, the recipient's attention is focused upon it. The same applies to the sub-headings; they are well laid out and clearly seen. If the different items had all been run together, although no doubt grammatically correct, they would not have been so easily read and understood.

Paragraphing and Setting Out

In the business letter dealing with quotations, inquiries, delivery dates and so on the writer can hardly go wrong in the setting out of the paragraphs, because each item will have a separate heading or paragraph. The danger is greater when we come to deal with the more general business letter and, of course, in social letters where information of a more interesting character is conveyed, often in greater detail.

I have already described the sentence to the beginner and a working description of a paragraph would be to say that it is composed of several sentences dealing with the same subject. This, however, must be qualified because one could write a ten-page letter composed of sentences dealing with the same subject and one paragraph of such a length would make a letter extremely difficult to follow as well as giving the reader no pause or break.

As a general working plan the letter writer should bear in mind that a paragraph should preferably be not more than about fifteen or at the most twenty lines, with an average of perhaps eight to ten lines as an ideal paragraph length. A letter composed of these average paragraphs is easy to read and follow, but this, however, is only a guide, and there is no fixed rule. A paragraph can vary from between one line to pages in length. One must, however, avoid new paragraphs merely for the sake of it, or on the other hand running two different subjects together because one paragraph may be a little short. In other words, do not be afraid of short paragraphs where necessary. Here is a letter written in paragraphs to show their uses.

I was delighted to hear from you that you all enjoyed your holiday on the Continent, and that you returned fit and well.

Now I have a bit of news which will no doubt interest you. We had a Grand Fancy Dress Ball at the Church Hall last Saturday. It was the biggest affair the village has seen for many years. Lady Templeton graced the gathering, appearing as Old Mother Hubbard—you never saw anyone look such a scream—and she had that moth-eaten old poodle of hers to complete the picture. Of course, the inevitable happened. Half-way through the evening Don Bates turned up as Dick Whittington with his evil-looking tom cat. Before five minutes had gone by the place was in an uproar with these two chasing round (the cat and dog, I mean, not Don and Lady Temp.). The M.C. had to turn them all out in the end—so undignified, my dear! However, all is quiet again now and the usual humdrum existence continues.

When are you and the children coming over again? Do write to me soon and tell me when you can manage a week-end. I am so longing to see you. Good-bye for now.

The above shows the use of paragraphs of different length and it would have been quite permissible to have broken the middle paragraph, which is rather long, at the words "Of course, the inevitable happened . . .", where a different note is introduced into the little narrative, although it is really not necessary with a paragraph of this length. It is largely a matter of choice and while care is taken to avoid too extensive a paragraph equally a new paragraph must not be started right in the middle of a subject and a suitable break must be chosen.

If you are writing to old people or to very young children, don't use too small a hand. Failing sight may create a difficulty for the former, while if you use larger letters, a child will find reading easier. Children also love the occasional drawn illustration, even if you are a poor artist! Both groups are usually keener to receive a letter than the average busy person.

5

Style

THERE is a good deal of confusion about style. Many people are not quite clear what it means. I think a good definition of it would be that it is the manner in which you, as an individual, express your thoughts. Therefore, do not let style be a bogy to you as it is to many people. I will go further and say that if you have good subject matter your style will largely look after itself. What might be called the "niceties of style" can, of course, be developed and are acquired perhaps by the wide reading of experienced authors, noting how they express their ideas and thoughts and in practice. The chief thing to remember about style is to keep your writing simple and straightforward because anything which is too involved and complicated is bad writing.

Here is an example of muddled style.

I have just seen Jackson about the forthcoming meeting and he has made various different suggestions about the place and time. We do not know whether the meeting will be large or small but it would probably be best to hold it in the

Wilson Rooms and Jackson thinks the time should be 8.30 not 7.30 otherwise there might not be room for everyone.

You can see at a glance that the writer of the above paragraph did not have clearly in mind what he wanted to convey. Let us analyse sentence by sentence. His first sentence is quite clear, but the second is very muddled; it should read thus:

We do not know whether the meeting will be large or small, so it will probably be best to hold it in the Wilson Rooms, otherwise there might not be accommodation for everyone. Jackson also thinks that the time should be 8.30 instead of 7.30.

This simple example shows the advantage of the short sentence for clarity.

Another important point is the avoidance of superfluous words and adjectives. In speaking it is sometimes necessary to repeat what has been said for effect and to use adjectives such as "very" to emphasize, but in writing it is wise to avoid any repetition as far as possible, the reason being simply that the written word can be read over again if necessary. One of the greatest faults of a letter writer is he who pumps one adjective from beginning to end. Wonderful day—wonderful food—wonderful sands. Imagine how irritating a letter of this kind can become. We can all remember being taught at school not to use the same word twice in the same sentence or even on the same page, but this is going rather far as quite often it is not worth while changing a word because it has been used a few lines above. Indeed, some writers employ repetition of a word for emphasis.

Much more important is the need to avoid repetition of information in a sequence of similar words. If one wishes to emphasize something it may be necessary to go over the ground again. Use different arguments and try to present the question from a different angle. There is much to be said for the old adage that "Brevity is the soul of wit", so not only keep out superfluous words but, more important, superfluous information. In a social letter, this does not mean you should omit detail, provided it is of interest.

Style alone, in the form of a lot of words correctly put together, can be boring in the extreme. In short, matter, rather than manner, is what matters. (Note repetition of the word matter for effect!) Have something to write and there will be little need to worry about how to write it. Style comes easily to those who have interesting facts to convey. Subtleties of method, lightness in style, humorous ways of writing and the like can soon be achieved by thought and practice and by studying the methods used by others.

But do not try and develop style. Your own is

probably far better than any which you may copy. Absorb ideas and constructions from well written books and the classics if you must, but do not consciously imitate. After all, however badly you may write, the recipient is more interested in you than in your attempts to impress by a style which is not part of you.

There is so much to do in the modern world – and so little time – that the day of the many-paged letter is almost over, except to friends and relatives in far-off lands.

Therefore one needs to acquire a crisp and compact style. One way to cultivate this is to study the short leaders in the more popular papers, and learn how they achieve effect and grip the interest.

Another method of improving your style is to read lots of the letters which appear in the daily press. These are usually of an extremely high standard, otherwise they would not get printed.

6

Dangers of the Written Word

THE wit who said, "Do right and fear no man; don't write and fear no woman", exaggerated. It is, however, true that many letters are written which in law undoubtedly provide grounds for libel, defamation of character or even breach of promise but of which, for a variety of reasons, nothing more is heard.

Let us first deal with libel. The word "libel" means any malicious or defamatory piece of writing and must be avoided at all costs, unless done under privilege.

It is also widely believed that the truth is not libellous, but this is not so; indeed, the truth is probably more dangerous than fictional libel. Let us imagine that my next-door neighbour had assaulted somebody twenty years ago and had received a term of imprisonment, in other words he had committed a crime and paid the legal penalty. It would be the truth if I should tell others in the neighbourhood that this man who had recently become my neighbour was an ex-convict, but you can see how unfair it would be to him and, in my opinion rightly, he could take action against me.

Libel, being written, is more punishable in law than slander on account of the permanency of the written word.

The letter beginning "I am writing to tell you what I think of you", and continuing to inform the recipient what you think of him, can be libellous, although addressed to the individual and not "published". The fact that it has been written assumes publication, although there are instances where statements can be made quite legally, if done in the proper manner.

Perhaps the most common example is a reference as to character or integrity; if something disparaging has to be said, provided it is done in good faith and without malice and headed "confidential and privileged" much can be written which would otherwise be actionable. It is, of course, essential for the envelope containing the information to be properly sealed and also marked "confidential", and carefully addressed to the correct recipient.

Another danger sometimes might be that well-meaning people would make a threat, but the law takes an extremely serious view of anything of this nature. The sort of thing I mean is this:

> If your son continues to pester my daughter kindly tell him I will come round and punch his nose.

After all, there is legal machinery for dealing with

people who pester others and I, personally, think the law in these matters is right, although many people who have never suffered under a threat might take the other view.

If such a letter has to be sent it can be done in a legal way, thus:

Confidential (envelope ditto)
I regret to inform you that your son has been pestering my daughter against her wishes, and I must insist that you stop him doing so. Naturally I would be very reluctant to have to put the matter into legal hands.

The last sentence might be unnecessary depending upon how serious the situation was. So long as you were sure and had some evidence that the young man was forcing his attentions on your daughter there could be no danger in such a letter. Of course, if the young man was grown up the letter would go to him and not to his parents.

Victims of Threats or Blackmail

In most instances by far the best advice is to ignore such letters, whether anonymous or not, except in the case of blackmail or serious threats. Blackmail is where money, or the equivalent or some service is demanded under threat of exposure. It matters not whether what the sender threatens to expose is true or false, the law takes a very grave view of the blackmailer. So, too, with any serious threat and in all such instances a reputable firm of lawyers should be consulted or the matter put into the hands of the police. The difficulty of the latter procedure is that the police might insist on taking some action, against your wishes; whereas, normally, a solicitor will be guided by your instructions.

In blackmail, where the threatened exposure happens to be some former indiscretion, it can, I believe, always be arranged that the victim's name need not appear in Press reports.

One needs to use common sense and judgement in these affairs. As I said above, often the least troublesome way of handling some letter written to you in the heat of the moment, is to forget it.

Pen Friends

Thousands of lonely people make use of pen-friend clubs which abound all over the world. In many instances the friendships resulting are innocent and genuine but the greatest care should be exercised. It is known that a number of people who use these clubs do so for their own selfish ends. It is usually better to make friends in a more conservative way.

Conclusion

The dangers of the written word, with which we are mainly concerned are less of a legal nature than of a social nature. There is no question that letters can be the cause of family squabbles and of serious differences, sometimes tragic, between friends purely owing to hasty action or misunderstandings. I shudder to think of the number of boy and girl friendships which have been ended because of some foolish letter.

The message of this short chapter is to advise the reader to be extremely careful in writing anything of a dangerous character and to be careful that the phrasing of the letter is such that it cannot be misunderstood. Letters should not be written in the heat of the moment, or, if they are, they should be laid aside and considered the next day. When something disagreeable has to be said to someone or about someone it is very much safer to do so verbally and in confidence and then, of course, even in speaking to a person one must avoid slander.

It must, of course, be realized that between understanding friends much can be written which could not be sent to comparative strangers. It is largely a question of knowing to whom you are writing, but the need for care is always present. Think twice before you write once.

Copyright

Whenever anything is spoken or written it automatically becomes copyright. Even in a private letter one must not quote others without permission and acknowledgement of the source. That is the legal position but, of course, if you are quoting in a letter what your wife said when she sat on a pin——.

Well, that's different!

Again, it is normal practice to quote brief extracts, using inverted commas, from various printed sources provided you are using them to explain some point or confirm some view you hold. Give the source of the extract, especially if it is a long one.

Quoting from another source in a letter is quite different from doing so in material which is going to be published for the public. The latter cannot be done safely without permission.

7

Samples of Easy Letters

The Thank You Letter

THE usual problem with the thank you letter is to be able to get it long enough. Of course, there is no necessity to do so, but it is nicer if one can, otherwise, it appears too businesslike.

Christmas/Birthday Gift

Thank you very much for remembering me with the beautiful fountain-pen. As you can see from my writing this pen has helped it greatly! I cannot think how you knew the type of nib which suits me, but obviously your research was excellent. Although I know you did not send it for that reason, this pen will remind me to write to you and my other friends more frequently and the ease with which it flows will make the task pleasant.

When you get time do write and tell me how your brother and his wife are getting on in Africa and how they are liking it out there.

I was very pleased to hear from Freeman that your firm are sending you out to New York on a business trip; I hope it will be successful and that you will have a good time.

Heartily reciprocating your good wishes for Christmas and the New Year.

Wedding Gift

John and I thank you most sincerely for your beautiful gift. It is one of the things we so much wanted but could not afford, and no one but you thought of it.

We will use it in the garden and on the many picnics which we hope to have, but what we also hope is that you will join us on some of these outings.

We got home from our honeymoon yesterday and there are so many things to be done. I know you will excuse this note being short. Again, many thanks and all good wishes from us both.

An Occasional Gift

On returning home from the office (after a tiring day) I was very thrilled to find that you had sent round a dozen eggs, but the thrill was even greater when my wife placed a dish of bacon and eggs before me for my supper.

For some weeks now I have been intending to send you some of our pippin apples, but I have not had the time to harvest them. I am hoping to pick them at the week-end and will try and bring some over to you on Monday evening about 8.30. Again thank you for thinking of us.

For a Service Rendered

How very kind of you to go to the trouble of bringing our dog back from Caterham; my husband and I do greatly appreciate what you have done.

Patch often wanders far afield but this time he seems to have wandered too far.

I enclose a postal order for £2 which we estimate it must have cost you to get here, but if it was more, please let us know as we would not wish you to be out of pocket.

Once again, thank you very much for your great kindness.

Sending a Gift

As I was reading the enclosed book I kept thinking how much it would amuse you and make you laugh, especially the part about bringing the logs in, because I know how far away from the house you store your logs. So many people have read *The Specialist* that I hope you are not one of them, but, somehow, I do not think it is the sort of book that you would buy although I am certain you will enjoy it.

Have fun at Xmas and may the New Year bring you everything that is good for you!

Inquiring for Accommodation

I have seen your advertisement in *The Lady* offering accommodation by the sea, and would be grateful if you would send me a brochure showing terms. I require a double bedroom for my wife and myself and two single rooms for my grown-up daughters from August 1st–14th inclusive.

When writing please mention if there is a bathing pool within a mile of your hotel and also if the hotel is licensed.

Will it be possible for us to bring our dog, which is a well house-trained fox terrier?

Arranging an Appointment

I wish to make an appointment to see you regarding the trust on which we are engaged. Any day after the 15th September up to the end of that month would suit me, so will you please pick a day and time and let me know and I will come to your house. After 6 p.m. would suit me best but I could manage earlier.

With kind regards.

Confirming an Appointment

Thank you for your letter of the 12th September, and the best day for me would be Monday, the 17th September at about 2.30 p.m. There is no need to acknowledge this if it suits you, so that unless I hear to the contrary I shall look forward to meeting you then.

Please be sure to bring the bank statements which I think you have.

Sending Enclosures

I enclose two invoices for decorating the three bedrooms and the dining-room of your home. You will notice that the amount works out at £4 more than our original estimate. The extra cost is because of the better quality paper which you decided upon while the work was in progress, but I thought I would mention it.

With compliments.

Advice

(a) Just a line to advise that I have dispatched a brace of pheasants and a hare to you this morning. They were shot on the 9th. (This could be on a postcard.)

(b) I hope to call at about 2.30 p.m. on Friday, November 23rd to tune your piano. If this date is inconvenient please let me know by return, but if convenient there is no need to reply.

Acknowledgements

Thank you very much for your cheque for the pulpit fund. This is particularly appreciated in these difficult times. The builders hope to begin the repairs next week.

Courtesy Letter

Many thanks for sending me the magazine about the new television set. I have read the article with great interest and I do appreciate your kind thought.

Simple Letters to Children

Try to write as simply and clearly as possible. Children always want facts to the bitter end, and are not interested in possibilities or probabilities. Never leave an incident unfinished, and try also to keep the syntax very simple. For small children it is advisable to print the letters as nowadays children are taught a disjointed writing first and find an adult scrawl very difficult to decipher.

Example

Dear John,

Many happy returns of the day. I am very sorry I have not been able to send you a present but Uncle John has been in bed with a cough and I have had to look after him. When I next go down to the shops I will pop into the first one I see and buy you something, so watch the postman each morning.

Our cat has had five kittens. Two are black and three white. They are still very weak and their eyes are closed. Next time you come to see us I expect they will be playing in the dining-room.

I must go and get Uncle John's lunch now.

Love,
Auntie Jane.

Apology Letter

I must write to apologize for the way I behaved at your party last night. I hope you will forgive me. The only excuse I can offer is that I had rather too much to drink; otherwise I am sure I would not have lost my temper.

I am sincerely sorry and will try never to do anything like it again. I hope you and Mrs. Brown can forgive me.

Thanks after being entertained

The telephone is widely used to say 'thank you' for parties, and even for gifts, but if somebody has taken a lot of trouble on your behalf, there is nothing better than a letter.

It was kind of you to ask me and Willy to spend the weekend at your farm. The break did me a lot of good, and Willy has hardly stopped talking about the pigs and the pony. We both loved every minute. Thank you so much.

When we got home . . .

8

Congratulations, Greetings, Sympathy and Invitations

I HAVE purposely not included the above headings in the previous chapter of easy letters because, as we all know, they are not always simple to write. The great difficulty with such letters is to avoid seeming insincere and to make them read as if the sender really meant every word. One must avoid sounding trite.

Congratulations

(a) I must write and congratulate you on having obtained your medical degree at so young an age. If all reports are correct we are deeply in need of more doctors so I have no doubt that you will easily find a good position. Are you thinking of specializing or are you going to stick to the good old family practitioner line? It always seems to me much better for a young man to concentrate on becoming a specialist later on as there is not quite so much "competition".

My wife and I would like very much if you

a

could come down and spend a week-end, if you have time. There are lots of good fish in the river! We are feeding them up!

(b) Well done! I am never quite sure whether to congratulate the mother or the father on these occasions, but judging by the most work done it is obviously to you that I must send the largest share of my hearty good wishes. Be sure and train your husband from the start in matters of baby welfare because by doing so you will have a much more peaceful life.

But seriously, I am delighted that you have got a girl and that you are both fit and well and look forward to seeing you in a week or two.

Greetings (Christmas)

I am enclosing the usual family Christmas card but that always seems such a lazy way of wishing a good friend a Merry Christmas.

I do miss shooting with you on Saturdays more than I can say, but I expect you get plenty of shooting in Africa and probably bigger targets than our local rabbits. When you have time please drop me a line and tell me conditions both of your work and play in Rhodesia. I have nothing much to report here—life goes on smoothly as usual, but I do send sincere greetings for Christmas and wish you the very best for the New Year.

Sympathy

These letters are very difficult to write although some people have a gift for it. For the majority it is better to keep the letter fairly short and not try to write too much. Many letters of sympathy are concerned with deaths, but of course other instances call for condolences from a minor accident to, perhaps, divorce. With all this type of letter care is necessary in case any double meaning is conveyed.

(a) My wife and I were greatly saddened this morning by reading in the *Telegraph* of your husband's death. There is so little one can say at such a time, but we do express our most sincere sympathy to you in your great bereavement.

In past years it was customary to write a much more lengthy letter dealing with certain aspects of the deceased's life and perhaps mentioning such matters as his long association with this or that but generally the message of sympathy is apt to be lost in words describing matters which are usually very obvious and therefore unnecessary. In such instances usually the simple sincere message meets the case best, although there are exceptions.

(b) I was very sorry to hear of the fire at your house and that you have lost everything. What a blow it must be to both of you after having so recently set up house. Do write and let us know what you are doing in the meantime, because if you are going into another house we can spare several chairs and a dining-room table which we have stored in the attic. I hope you won't mind my offering to lend these, but although they are perhaps not particularly attractive they might suit you until you get something. Do let me know if the above interests you; if not, don't trouble to reply as you must be busy.

Informal Invitations

With every year we are becoming less formal and I have no doubt that very soon the formal invitation will be reserved for the Lord Mayor's Banquet and the like and the rest of us will ring each other up or send a simple letter. In fact, even now the majority of invitations are done in this way. I will therefore give a few sample invitations.

(a) We are having a few friends round to bridge on Wednesday night (2nd October) at 8.30 and would be very glad if you could come. It is an informal affair—lounge suits; there will only be about four tables.

(b) We would all like if you could spend a week with us during the second half—preferably the last week—of August, arriving on the

24th. I am having Bill over from Ireland so we should have lots of fun together. I think the only things to bring are 1, your bicycle; 2, your bathing-suit; and 3, your airgun; otherwise we have everything here. I do hope you can come.

(c) I am wondering if you will be in London during the first week of next month and, if so, whether you would come out with me for a meal and cinema. I would suggest either Monday the 7th or Wednesday the 9th and that we meet at Piccadilly Circus underground station (entrance to Swan & Edgar's). Please let me know as soon as you can, mentioning what time you can be there (5.30 p.m. would suit me).

Formal Invitations

There is no need to be too much afraid of the formal invitation. The only real reason for their use is that where a few dozen have to be sent out it does save writing letters by hand. It is quite correct to write a card in long hand, but the usual method is to have a printed invitation card, which is rather like a postcard. These cards can either be specially printed or bought for the purpose at your stationer's with blank spaces for the names to be filled in. As they are printed matter they can be sent in an unsealed envelope although it is probably wiser to send them in a closed envelope for safety and quicker delivery.

Wedding Invitation

MR. AND MRS. DENNIS CLARK
request the pleasure of the company of

Mr & Mrs Wilson

at the marriage of their daughter

Katherine Angela

WITH

MR. GERALD K. SWINDON
at St. Matthew's Parish Church
on Saturday, 18th May, 19- -
at 2.30 o'clock

3 MERE CLOSE   R.S.V.P.
BATH

Bridge/Cocktail Invitation

Mr. and Mrs. Williamson request the pleasure of Miss Jackson's company on Wednesday, 12th December, 19- -, at 6.30 p.m.

BRIDGE.

24 Woodland Avenue,   R.S.V.P.
Woking, Surrey.

Everyone knows that R.S.V.P. means please reply and comes from the French phrase,
"Répondez s'il vous plaît".

"At Home" Cards

These can be bought with the words "At Home" and "R.S.V.P." already printed and are filled in as shown in the accompanying illustration.

Mr. J. R. Clark

The Misses Mary & Jean Smith

at Home

Saturday, 18th December, 19

R.S.V.P.

Dancing   3, The Close, Hastings,

8.30–12.30   Sussex.

Informal Acceptances (and *Refusals*)

These simply mean an ordinary letter accepting or refusing an invitation, which can be written in the following way:

(a) Thank you very much for inviting my wife and me to play bridge with you on Thursday evening. We shall be very pleased indeed to come along and look forward to seeing you. With kind regards.

(b) Thank you very much for your letter inviting me to spend Saturday week fishing with you, but owing to a previous engagement—office tennis competition—I shall not be able to come. I should very much like to go fishing with you some other Saturday and any one in July would suit me if you can fit it in. I hope you catch lots of fish next week.

Tight lines!

While it is quite all right to refuse an invitation on the grounds of a previous engagement it is always more friendly, I think, to say what the other engagement is, if possible.

Formal Acceptances

Wedding (*written by hand on good note-paper*)

Mr. and Mrs. S. M. Brown thank Mr. and Mrs. Dennis Clark for their kind invitation to the marriage of their daughter Katherine Angela at St. Matthew's Church on Saturday, 18th May, and have much pleasure in accepting.

or

and deeply regret having to refuse owing to a previous engagement.

Bridge/Cocktails

Mr. and Mrs. Jack White have much pleasure in accepting Mr. and Mrs. Gray's kind invitation to bridge on Wednesday, 24th November, at 7.30 p.m.

Where the friendship is long standing because a formal invitation card has been sent, that does not imply that a *formal* acceptance or refusal must be sent. Particularly in the case of a refusal although a formal refusal card or note-paper may be included, it is a gesture of friendship to write an informal letter as well, explaining why one cannot be present.

Nowadays telephoning is cheaper than writing, so many more parties are arranged by 'phone. The post, however, is still used for most of the larger affairs. For one thing, the invitation card looks nice on the mantelpiece of the recipient, and acts as a reminder of the date.

9

Introductions and Testimonials

Introductions

ODDLY enough, it would appear a very easy matter to write a letter of introduction and the actual writing of the letter is not difficult, but what the sender has to realize is that often the greatest importance is attached to such correspondence. Your letter of introduction addressed to a business man on behalf of an acquaintance might result in his obtaining an important position, whereas your original letter might merely have been to introduce the two parties with a view to some small matter such as the supply of curtains. In other words, considerable importance might be attached to the fact that you had gone to the trouble of giving an introduction and assumption might be made that because you had done so you knew the party to be absolutely reliable, which might not be the case. Therefore, always take great care as to the exact wording of your introduction so that no false assumptions can be arrived at by the ultimate recipient.

I will give you several sample letters of introductions. The first is introducing an acquaintance who wishes to open an account with my bank, and is addressed to the manager.

This letter is to introduce Mr. Lewis who, I understand, wishes to open an account with you. He is an acquaintance of mine whom I have known for some weeks and I trust you will be able to help him.

On the other hand, here is a letter of introduction for someone whom I have known for many years and found to be a person of integrity and reliability.

This letter is to introduce Mr. Kendall who, I understand, wishes to open an account with you. I have known him for nearly ten years and always found him to be a man of integrity. I trust you will be able to do business together to your mutual advantage.

Here is a letter introducing someone who is moving to a new town.

This letter is to introduce Miss Jameson who is leaving here to live in Dundee. I have known her for several years and as she has no friends in Dundee I am taking the liberty of asking you if you can help her to meet some people as it is always difficult for anyone going to a strange town. I know you will do your best for her. Many thanks.

The next sample letter introduces someone seeking employment.

I am taking the liberty of writing to introduce Mr. Willis who is looking for a job connected with the printing trade. I have not known him for long, but have every reason to believe that you would find him entirely satisfactory should you have any opening for which his particular qualifications would be suitable.

As I do not know many people in the printing trade, perhaps if you have nothing for him you could give him the names of one or two other firms in the district to whom he might apply.

Thanking you very much for your help in this matter.

There are various other kinds of introduction, such as someone going to live in the district being introduced to the local tradesmen, and this can either be done by a simple letter or a telephone call.

Testimonials or References

It would be impossible to overstress the importance of the wording of a testimonial or reference, because a very great deal can depend upon it. The ordinary reference from a commercial firm is not worth much unless the recipient knows something about the writer of the reference. I refer here to the testimonial which a person leaving takes with him. The reason for this is simply that it is always assumed that a good deal of praise is put into the letter, possibly more out of kindness than merit.

The more valuable reference is the one which is obtained by the prospective employer writing direct to the former employer asking any particular questions he might wish answered. Indeed, this latter type of reference is extremely valuable, and if the two employers are situated near each other the matter is generally dealt with on the telephone. As a general rule, employers are very fair minded and give a square deal.

One of the reasons why I *personally* never attach any great value to a testimonial is that although a person may have done badly in a previous job it does not follow that he will do badly in the next position. Conditions of employment may vary and in the nature of personal relationships there are often employees who cannot work satisfactorily for one man, but who can for another. Again, sometimes if an employee has not done very well in a previous job he has learnt his lesson and will do much better in the new task.

The Writing of References

Those who are asked to write a reference should be guided by the following points:

(i) Absolute accuracy.
(ii) Brevity.

The old-fashioned reference which dwelt on length of service, qualities of character and so on for several pages is probably rarely read and business people today really want a crisp summary of the individual concerned.

I give below some references for good employees who have left for various reasons:

(a) Miss Kelly has left our employment as a shorthand typist as she is moving her home away from this area. We have found her first class in every respect.

(b) Mr. Gale has left our employment to better his position. He has been in charge of our order department for three years and given us complete satisfaction. He leaves us with our best wishes for his future.

(c) It gives us great pleasure to write that Mr. Black has been our sales manager for three years and is leaving us because our business has been sold. He is a man of enormous energy and initiative and we have no doubt whatever that he will excel in any new position he undertakes.

So much for these comparatively easy references, but we now come to the problem of giving a reference to a person less satisfactory as an employee. This is a very difficult matter because naturally an employer does not like to condemn someone who may have been unsatisfactory in the past. The best line to take with somebody who has not been too bad is to write something like the following suggestion :

Mr. Green is leaving our employment because he wishes a higher salary than we feel able to pay. He has been with us four years and we have always found him trustworthy and wish him success in his future.

We now come to the much more difficult instance of the employee who has been dishonest and thoroughly unsatisfactory. The best way to deal with this matter is to refuse to give a reference but to say that you are willing to supply one to a prospective employer. The probability is that the individual will never give your name because he would not expect a good reference and if he is dishonest he will probably make up some story or provide a bogus reference. In passing I might mention that all the people, and there have been a few, who have most seriously swindled me were the ones who provided the most wonderful references as to their integrity etcetera.

Privileged and Confidential References

In giving an adverse reference regarding an employee one is entitled to state the facts fully but carefully, provided the letter is addressed to the inquirer personally and headed "Privileged and in strictest confidence". The envelope should be marked "Strictly confidential".

Let me say here that it is always much better to give an adverse reference by word of mouth than in writing and the line to take is to tell the truth about the person, but without malice, as the legal position is always somewhat uncertain. Even in a privileged letter if anything was said which was out of malice or spite, however tempted one might be, the legal position might prove very dangerous.

Do not give a bad reference on the telephone as people can "listen-in" although fortunately it is rarely done.

One can hardly be too careful in such matters.

Carbon Copies

It is normally only necessary to keep copies of letters which contain details or figures to which you may later wish to refer or of some important matter of which a record is essential.

10

The Technique of the Longer Letter

MANY people find the writing of a long letter, whether social or business, a very difficult matter. I have bracketed the social and business letters together because in practice there is no great difference. It is true that the commercial letter may require more thought and more careful setting out if it contains specifications or prices and so on, but a great many business letters do not have these details and are very much the same, so far as the problem of writing them goes, as the social letter.

Perhaps the most important thing which the beginner has to learn is that a letter, to be really effective, should be written more or less as one would speak. In other words, do not sit down and look at the paper and feel "Oh! dear, what can I *write*", but just begin writing the letter as if you were talking to the person. In this way the letter becomes what is termed "live".

Another point to be remembered is that if you put yourself in the place of the recipient and try to think of the things he would like to find in the letter you will get ideas as to what to write.

In these long letters try to avoid putting in extra words just for the sake of length, otherwise the letter is apt to be boring. Also remember that it does greatly add to interest if you can quote what friends have said or tell of a humorous happening to yourself or to someone else, as well as giving the usual particulars of places. In other words, human interest is generally more exciting than anything else.

Another factor creating a good letter is the avoidance of too much about the obvious and the filling of the letter with as much unusual information as possible, particularly with material which will be of especial interest to the person receiving the letter.

A good method of learning how to write chatty letters is to read what I believe is called the gossip column in most daily and evening newspapers. Journalists who write these articles appear to do so very easily and you will notice how easy their material is to read, but this is the result of long experience and judgement as to what interests the majority and also the way in which it is set down. That is why such journalistic jobs are highly paid. The careful study of the methods used will be most helpful in your own letter writing.

Here is a sample longer letter from a man to his friend about his holiday.

A Social Letter

This will come as a surprise to you, because I did not tell you I was going to Aroza (Switzerland) for a holiday. I did not know myself until a few days ago, but the doctor ordered me to have a change on account of an attack of coughing—so here I am in Aroza.

To me it is quite amazing—the snow is twenty-four inches deep and no slush or mud such as we get in England. What is particularly wonderful is that although everything is covered with snow or ice one does not feel at all cold; in fact I was out today without a coat.

On arrival four days ago I went to the local Ski School and borrowed skis because I wanted to learn. They told me that I could have a seven-day course, but as I am only here for seven days I said I wanted to learn more quickly but was assured that was impossible. For my first days I stayed on what are called the nursery slopes with a crowd of other people learning to ski under the expert instruction of a local guide, but after the first two days I found this too slow for me so decided to join a party going up the mountainside.

They make everything very easy for the visitor *going up* even to the extent of a special "lift" which takes you to the mountain-top and which I was delighted to use. Once at the top I decided to abandon caution and risk my life in going down the slopes. Unless you have done some skiing you cannot believe what a wonderful feeling it is. Forty miles an hour, or whatever speed it is one goes at, seems like 500 because you are so near the soft snow. My trouble was that I had not learned properly and did not quite know how to stop or turn, with the result that I had to hope for the best at all times. On one occasion doing, I think, about 50 m.p.h. I managed to turn round a bend and found myself heading straight for a group of people talking. I did not know how to stop, but shouted to them to get out of the way and fortunately they stood aside, leaving about 2 feet for me to get through. They still do not know it, but it was mere luck that got me through this space. As I did so I suddenly found myself at the top of a small hillock which left me no alternative, as I could not stop, but to jump. I need hardly tell you that the jump was a complete failure and I found myself buried under about three feet of snow, but glad to be still alive if not kicking! ...

I have purposely not finished this letter, but it shows the sort of thing.

Here is an example of a business letter and the reader will notice that the technique employed is not so very different. During this letter I want to show how in writing quite a lot can be said which might be offensive to the recipient unless some tact is used. Let us imagine that this is a reply to a request from one of my agents for a thousand catalogues to send round to his bookseller customers.

A Business Letter

Many thanks for your letter asking for a thousand catalogues, which I am sending to you separately.

I am sure you will not mind my pointing out that I do not think posting catalogues round to customers is the best way to sell books. Nine out of ten of them probably go straight into the waste paper basket and I think you would be better advised to ask your travellers to carry some of the catalogues with them, and also to carry a selection of at least half a dozen of the books themselves.

May I also say that in our experience if the travellers were to read the books or at least read parts of them and examine them very carefully they will get much better results. After careful examination they will begin to appreciate the difference between our books and those of competitors. When showing the books to the buyers if they open them at the interesting figures and drawings or show the comprehensive contents pages or indexes, depending on the book, I am quite certain far better results will be obtained.

You mention in your letter that in spite of heavy advertising and circularizing with catalogues and leaflets you were finding trade extremely difficult. May I say that I regard most of this advertising as a waste of money. You can justifiably turn round and say to me, well why do you go in for it so much yourself? My answer is, I too am a sucker.

I trust you will agree with me about showing the actual books to the trade and if so, on hearing from you, I shall be pleased to send sample copies for your travellers.

Remember, you can write an entirely different kind of letter to someone whom you know well and understand than you can send to a stranger.

When you don't know the person, you must think harder if you want to make the letter readable and interesting.

With old friends you can discuss subjects which you know are of interest, and it is always easy to send news of mutual acquaintances. If you find yourself 'stuck', don't persevere too long, but leave the letter for a few hours, or even overnight. When you return to it you may well find that fresh ideas flow easily.

11

Answering a Letter

ONE would hardly imagine it necessary to write a chapter on answering a letter, but from a long experience of both having done so and having received answers to my own letters I regard this as one of the most important chapters of the book.

The first rule about answering a letter is obviously to answer it and this is where so many people go wrong. Frequently in social letters and more often in business letters there may be three, six or even a dozen different matters for attention. What so often happens is that the reply covers about half of them, but the other points raised are ignored, which is, to say the least of it, extremely exasperating. The safe method is to have the letter you are replying to in front of you and as you reply to the various questions or matters raised to draw a line through the relative part of the letter you are answering. In this way you can see at a glance when you have replied completely.

Replying to a letter affords, of course, an excellent opportunity for writing about something else and particularly in the business world I have found many people who lose wonderful opportunities by failure in this respect. Thus, for example, a customer writing to inquire when some particular goods will be ready affords an excellent opening of offering him something else as well.

In my other book, entitled, *Business Letters, Contracts and Etiquette*, I have dealt much more fully with this subject than space allows here, but one thing can be said—the vast majority of business men completely fail to realize what can be achieved by letter writing.

While dealing with answering letters, normally, especially with commercial correspondence, the reply should if possible be sent by return mail, as doing so gives a very good impression. In social letters there is usually less urgency, but again there is nothing so easy as putting off the writing of a letter and days of delay are liable to spread into months.

There is also the letter which is better left unanswered, as this is sometimes the best and easiest way of dealing with a very tricky matter. As this is another story I shall deal with it in the next chapter.

12

The difficult or "Tricky" Letter

I WOULD like to begin this chapter with the advice that when you have a difficult or "tricky" letter to write the best thing is, if you can, not to write it but to deal with the matter verbally. This is much safer because of the possibility of misunderstandings, and again in a verbal "encounter" you are more likely to know where you are without delay. The time elapsing between the sending of, and the reply to, a letter dealing with an important or difficult matter can be very worrying. There do, however, arise occasions where something has to be put in writing or a serious matter dealt with by correspondence.

In writing such letters remember the following points:

(i) Do not write until you have calmly considered.

(ii) Always be courteous and as brief as possible.

(iii) Be patient and, if necessary, persistent.

(iv) Don't worry *after* you have made your decision.

Below are given several examples.

To a neighbour regarding a troublesome dog

I have already spoken twice to you about your dog coming into my garden and frightening the children. I must ask you again to keep your dog under proper control and make sure that it does not come on to my premises, otherwise I shall be forced to take legal action, which, needless to say, I would regret.

Request for permission

After much hesitation, because of a natural British reluctance to ask favours I suppose, I am taking the liberty of writing to inquire if you would be so kind as to let me shoot the rabbits on your farm. You can rest assured that if you granted me permission I would not abuse it by coming too often; but would confine my visits to not more than once a month. Should I be successful in getting any rabbits I will be very pleased to share them with you if you would care to have them. I enclose a stamped addressed envelope for your kind reply.

The secret, if it is a secret, in asking permission is to be courteous in your approach and people are often delighted to grant such favours.

To an Insurance Company

This is a letter in reply to an insurance company's

communication declining to pay £10 for a coat which has been completely destroyed by fire and offering £3.

In reply to your letter offering £3 compensation against the coat which was recently burned and which had been bought two months ago for £10, I must ask you to reconsider the matter.

In twenty-one years I have never made a claim and have paid you in premiums many hundreds of pounds. Do you consider your offer of £3 against a coat worth £10 is fair treatment? I did not claim the larger sum with any intention of entering into negotiation for its reduction, because the coat had only been worn twice and was obviously still worth its original value, or within a few shillings of it.

Unless you send the £10 within the next week or ten days my policy will be transferred to another company and a writ will be served upon your company.

I await your reply and hope it will contain an explanation that some mistake has been made by your office.

It might be mentioned that unless you really intend to issue a writ do not make the threat. In other words, never indicate that you will do something unless you are resolved to do it.

Asking for Payment

I have often wondered how many accounts rendered have never been paid because of lack of patience. It is quite true that the man who receives an overdue account ought to reply promptly and say what he can do if he cannot pay the full amount, but unfortunately these hard-up people are either so worried or by nature so discourteous that they often do not trouble to reply, with the result that tempers are apt to become frayed and "good money thrown after bad", as the saying is.

When a statement of account is sent out if it is overdue a short note can be added to it asking for a remittance by an early post. The following month the wording can be stronger, for example, "As this account is now long overdue please remit by return." If these normal methods are unavailing then a letter can be sent. Here is a sample:

Confidential (also mark envelope "Confidential").

Your account is now eight months old and I have requested payment on several occasions. What annoys me more than the fact that you have not paid the full amount or part of it is the complete silence with which you treat my requests for payment. If there is some difficulty which prevents you from paying this account at the moment will you be good enough to notify me of it and I will see what can be done to extend the terms. I do feel, however, that you should make an effort to pay at least 25% of the account right away and make a promise of dates for the payment of the balance.

Kindly reply by return.

If this letter does not have any result after a few weeks a more strongly worded letter can be sent.

Confidential (also mark envelope "Confidential").

I am still without any reply to my letter of the (insert date) and this is very surprising. I must ask you firmly to make payment of at least half of the amount outstanding within the next fourteen days. As a matter of fact, I have some very heavy commitments to meet myself and it is essential that I receive your payment before (insert date). I await your reply.

If the date passes without any payment then after another few days yet another letter can be sent in even stronger language and it could conclude with such a phrase as this:

You are leaving me no alternative but to take the strongest possible legal action. Kindly reply within seven days.

Notice that this does not commit you as to when you will take the legal action and as solicitors are expensive, unless the amount is very large or you have good reason to think that the people could easily pay it, it would probably be wise to drop the matter for a time until you feel the chance of payment is better. For example, if you are dealing with a shop-keeper it might be wise to wait till immediately after Christmas when he is likely to have some money in the till, or if your account is with a builder you might possibly hear of his having carried out a large contract and if you can time your next letter to coincide with some payments you believe he has received then it might stand a better chance.

One of the best ways of obtaining money is quiet persistence over a long period. Although in many cases letters may have to be written, where it is possible a personal visit is usually more successful. A note announcing that you will call personally on a certain date, say a week or two hence, often obtains excellent results. A writ or a solicitor is, of course, the final resort but in my experience the methods outlined above are usually successful.

Everyone should keep a carbon copy of all important letters for possible future reference. It should hardly be necessary to add that before signing anything it should be read over carefully.

13

The Love Letter

IN an earlier chapter I have mentioned that some care is necessary in letters passing between people of the opposite sex and as boys and girls become older the danger is increased; I refer mainly to the risk of causing unnecessary pain or hurting the feelings of another. In this matter it is commonly felt that only girls have feelings and men are devoid of them. Why this belief should prevail is one of those mysteries better left without discussion, but the truth undoubtedly is that a man's feelings are just as liable to be hurt as those of a girl, the pain being none the less because he receives little public sympathy.

Perhaps in no field of letter writing are the opportunities for achievement greater. Between people who are in love or between two people one of whom is in love with the other, the letter does, on occasion, provide an opportunity.

To deal with the more straightforward type of letter between lovers or engaged couples, in a surprising number of cases such people are separated by hundreds of miles and about the only way they can get to know each other is through the post. In a case where there is mutual understanding there should be no danger of misunderstanding and the letters can be long and filled with interesting material. There is one warning which might be issued, and that is the danger of being too passionate in ink because there is always the risk of misunderstanding or of the letters getting into the hands of someone for whom they were not intended. It is equally true that if a love letter is too cool the recipient might also misunderstand, so that a happy medium must be struck. Brief mention might be made, however, of the use of the letter under circumstances in which, shall we say, the man has fallen in love with the girl but the affair is still in its early stages.

Often the letter could be used for invitations or for enclosing some small Christmas or birthday gift and in this way it could help to increase a friendship which might ripen into something more. Once again, however, it is necessary to warn against the danger that any expression of love on the man's part may scare the girl away. For some reason a great many people are afraid of any expression of passion in a letter, especially between people who may not know each other very well, even though the one might imagine himself to be in love with the other.

In the case of a girl who has met a man she would like to know better the letter again offers her an opportunity to invite him out to a picnic, dance or party and so on, which might be difficult by other means such as the telephone.

There are one or two very important things to remember about love letters. One, I have already stressed, namely not to set the pace of the affair too fast. Another risk is one which, looked at in cold blood, may seem ridiculous but which nevertheless happens. Quite often a young man meets a girl on holiday and at the end of the holiday starts writing her not only every day but by every post. Those who have been in love will realize how difficult it is to be separated, but still some restraint is wise and I have known many a girl and boy friendship break down because—usually the man—wrote far too many letters and simply overwhelmed the girl and frightened her away. As a rule, men fall in love quickly, girls more slowly.

We have all read in the papers about the evidence of love letters and cases of breach of promise. But fortunately today the breach of promise case is a rarity. Despite the fact that you probably will not have to face a court and jury over it, it is nevertheless most unwise to declare your love or propose marriage until you are sure that you have met the right mate and although the love letter has its uses it is not the ideal way to make a proposal and, indeed, a proposal by letter is much easier to decline than one made in suitable and proper surroundings.

The breaking off of an engagement is more common today than in former times and here a

D

letter sometimes forms the best way of terminating an affair which is obviously heading for disaster. Perhaps the most important thing to remember if this has to be done is to write as nice a letter as possible in the circumstances.

This brings me to the subject of lovers' quarrels, which are alleged to be very common. One thing is certain, that it is most unwise to pick quarrels in letters. Personally, I think it is unwise to quarrel in any circumstances, but all facts indicate that quarrelling by letter is just about the height of folly. Letters are always liable to be misunderstood and something *said* in a heated moment may be forgotten more easily than the same thing *written* in a heated moment.

Sample "Love Letters"

From a girl who has met a young man on holiday whom she likes but who, although friendly, has shown no special interest in her. She rightly feels if he could get to know her better he *might* one day fall in love.

I remember when we met you mentioned that you were interested in music and that you played the piano. I hope you will not mind my taking the liberty of inviting you to join a music club which a friend and I are starting at the end of next month. There is no subscription or anything like that, it being all very informal and, we hope, friendly. I do hope you don't mind my writing to you and that you will join.

Notice there is NO indication of any affection which, if initiated by the girl, would be out of place as well as foolish. In our parents' time such a letter from a girl to a man would have been poor etiquette, but etiquette, like most customs, changes with the years.

Now a letter from a man to a girl breaking off a friendship which, although not an engagement, had reached the love affair stage.

I have been very worried since we met, especially on your account, but also on my own, and I think the fairest thing is for me to write and tell you about it at once. I might as well come to it, in the last three weeks I have done a lot of thinking and reached the conclusion that I am not the right man for you. For a time I thought we were suited, but on our last few days out together several things I did—especially over the drinks—obviously annoyed you and I will not deny one or two of your actions irritated me.

I think, and I'm sure you will agree, our best plan by far is to end our friendship now. I hope I have not hurt you too much by what was, perhaps, rather rash behaviour on my part. Please believe me in wishing you everything good for the future.

The next letter is from a girl to a man ending a long engagement.

I hardly know how to start this letter, because it is written on a matter about which I never imagined I should have to write. John, dear, will you ever forgive me if I ask you to release me from my engagement to marry you. My heart is broken on your account, because I do know how much you love me.

You remember when you first proposed to me and I refused—well, I was not sure then that you and I were suited, but your kindness and patience, in the end, won me over but my acceptance was, I now think, more logical than emotional. I realized then, as I do now, that you will make a wonderful husband, but I now know I am not the best girl for you.

Yes, there is someone else and that is what has brought the matter to a head. Do you remember meeting Howard at our office dance? Well, on Fridays he has been motoring me home as he passes my house on his way. I have always been attracted to him but never thought he had *any* interest in me. It was probably very wrong to let him motor me home, but I could not resist it and I hope you can forgive me.

The rest of the story is that on Friday he blurted out that he has been madly in love with me since he first saw me and he questioned me so closely on whether I was sure that I loved you and that you and I suited each other, that I am afraid I admitted I was not sure. . . .

What more can I say, John, except that I think Howard and I will hit it off perfectly. Write to me and tell me what I am to do for I am worried. I am sorry and will always remember. I can't write more now until I hear from you.

14

Applying for a Job

Replying to Advertisements

ONCE again emphasis can be given to keeping your letter short and to the point. Before replying, read the advertisement with great care and see that all the information requested is supplied in your answer. A very long letter giving vast details of your past and present life probably counts against you. I remember once advertising for a secretary and receiving over nine hundred replies, the longest of which was thirty-five pages. It was thirty-four pages too long.

Here are one or two sample advertisements with what I consider proper replies given beneath:

(a) *Advertisement*

Young man under twenty-five with good education required. Applicants should have mechanical aptitude as the work requires instruction and training with special machinery. Write giving full details of education and salary required. Box XYZ.

Reply

In reply to your advertisement in today's *Telegraph*, I have been interested in anything mechanical since childhood and have a workshop at home in which I have built various mechanical models. Since leaving my Grammar School eight years ago, I have been employed with the A.T.G. Engineering Co., but next month the firm are closing the branch at which I work, so that I am seeking a new position. I am twenty-three years old and was educated at Penfold Grammar School, where I secured the school certificate. As to salary, my present employers are paying me £x a week, but if the work you are offering is interesting and has some prospects I feel sure that this matter could be settled to our mutual agreement. I shall be glad to attend for an interview at any time should you so desire.

(b) *Advertisement*

Cook-housekeeper required for 8 people for flat. Dog kept. Good wages to suitable person. London. Box A.B.C.

Reply

I am pleased to apply for the position of cook-housekeeper offered in today's *Telegraph*. I am thirty-two years of age and since leaving school have held three positions as cook-housekeeper and can bring with me references from each job. I received my training at the Atholl Crescent Cooking School in Edinburgh and hold their diploma. Although I am at present employed I am anxious to obtain a position in London. My present salary is £x per week, but I would like an advance on this as I expect living in London will be more costly, this, however, could be discussed at any interview which I would be pleased to attend. I am very fond of dogs and hope to hear that this application has received your favourable attention.

(c) *Advertisement*

Representative required for London area by paper manufacturer. Must have connection and experience. Reply stating age, experience and salary. Box LMN.

Reply

I am applying for the position of sales representative in the London area as advertised. I am at present employed in a Government job which is mainly clerical, but as I was originally trained in the paper business I am most anxious to return to it. I am twenty-six years old and have over eight years' experience in the paper industry, which I obtained with

Messrs. Bates & Coal Ltd., but none of this experience was as a salesman. I have always been anxious to become a representative and would like very much to have the opportunity of training with you as I believe I could give satisfaction. In view of my lack of experience as a representative I am prepared to start at the small salary of £x a week, during training. I hope to hear that I may attend for an interview. I am dead keen.

(d) *Advertisement*

Director of City publishing house requires experienced shorthand typist. This position is one which offers scope for a keen girl with initiative. Reply with usual details. Box OPQ.

Reply

In reply to your advertisement in today's *Telegraph*, I was trained at the Grey Secretarial College and since leaving have been employed for five years as secretary to the managing director of Messrs. Timms & Butcher. I am certain my present employer would be agreeable to giving me a reference and my sole reason for wishing to leave is that I would like to get into the publishing business as it has always interested me greatly. I am twenty-three years old and unmarried and

would be willing to accept £x per week,
which is the salary I am now obtaining. I can
attend an interview at any time on hearing
from you. I am really keen.

There is no doubt, of course, that many positions
are filled which are never advertised. Sometimes
one hears of jobs which are open or likely to be
open and a visit to the employer may prove successful. In other cases a letter may have to be
written and, as with the foregoing letters, it should
be kept short and give brief but full particulars.
The letter could be composed in a variety of ways,
and here is an example:

I have heard from a friend that you are likely
to be requiring an invoice-clerk and I am
taking the liberty of offering my services. I
give here particulars of my previous experience:

The particulars can then be listed and that is all
there is to it. Conclude with: "I await your kind
reply and enclose a self-addressed envelope."

In other cases someone may move into a new
district and wish to secure a job in a particular
trade. The best way is probably to write, if there
are not too many of them, to the firms in the trade
you wish to enter in the locality and such a letter
could be in the following manner:

I have just moved into this district from Dorset and am anxious to secure employment in the grocery business. I give full particulars of my previous experience in this trade:

you could conclude:

I shall be glad to hear if there is any opening in your firm for which I might be suitable, or failing that if you can give me the name of any other firm to whom you think it might be worth while my writing. I enclose a reply envelope and thank you in anticipation.

15

Publicity and Sales Letter

IN a book of general letter writing only a limited space can be given to this subject which would really be more suitable to a book on business letters.

One of the great difficulties with both sales letters and publicity letters is to know whether they are worth while. In other words, a manufacturing concern might send out tens of thousands or even hundreds of thousands of sales letters and the result instead of being sales might be final ruin on account of the heavy cost of envelopes, stamps, paper, printing, etc. In the same way publicity may sometimes prove very costly, but there is no doubt that a certain number of sales letters are essential in any business and that used with care they can be the means of bringing great success. Where so much money is lost in sending out sales letters is when they are broadcast to all and sundry where the wastage by falling on "barren ground" is enormous, but on the other hand if you are selling stair carpet and can arrange for your letters to reach people who are about to be married then you are more likely to find a market. As a matter of fact it is true that a number of commercial houses do send sales letters to a list of people whose engagements are announced in the national Press.

There are, of course, two distinct kinds of sales letters. The first is more of a circular to a variety of people who may or may not be interested in the product; and then there is what might be termed the sales letter proper, which is a letter sent out to people who are extremely likely to buy. This last category is, of course, one of the most important for the commercial man. They vary from the special offer letter sent round to the firm's active list of customers to the reply to an inquiry.

I give below one example of the circular type of letter and here it is wise to mention that wherever possible such letters command more respect when individually typed and signed than when produced on some type of duplicating machine.

Special Offer

We have a large stock of very fine 9cm x 2cm Finnish whitewood flooring and as we require warehouse space we are anxious to move this at once. The normal market price for the flooring is . . . per square metre, but for all orders received within the next two weeks we are prepared to sacrifice the material at . . . per square metre. We may mention that the market price of this flooring is very firm and that our offer is made subject to prior sale.

We trust you can help us to move this material

and at the same time secure a quite exceptional bargain.

This sales letter contains the elements of surprise, coming as it does out of the blue, and gives the impression, which is an honest one, that the buyer will receive a bargain that he is unlikely to be able to repeat. Putting a time limit on the offer also encourages him to fix up an order, because otherwise the matter might be left aside and forgotten.

As explained above, many sales letters are really openings made by the sales manager in reply to an inquiry from a client. It is here that the writer's initiative has great scope. For example, a shop might be inquiring for a special size of women's shoes and in addition to replying to the inquiry an opportunity could be engineered to make an offer of some other goods likely to interest that particular shop, so that two or more orders may result instead of just one.

Publicity

Very few people in the commercial world fully appreciate the immense value of free publicity. Let us put it this way for clarity. An advertisement in a national daily of 3″ × 2″ may easily cost £80, whereas editorial space of the same size may cost nothing. It is a generally accepted view that the latter type of publicity has a far greater selling effect than an advertisement, the reason being that probably twice as many people read the text of a newspaper in preference to the advertisements, and that the advertisement is very often viewed as being prejudiced whereas the editorial space is likely to be accepted at its face value.

Make no mistake, publicity of this nature is by no means easy to obtain because newspapers, by the nature of things, have to be run for profit and if the editors of the different sections gave away too much free publicity the advertisement revenue would possibly fall seriously. This free publicity is, of course, of high value to a commercial house, but it is also very valuable to people in the public eye such as actors, clergymen, doctors, professional golfers and the like. Of course, medical men and members of some professions have to be rather careful in case a charge of advertising is levelled against them by their associations. Especially in some of the Sunday newspapers one notices many articles by clergymen and there is no question that these bring great benefit to the writers apart from immediate financial gain. When you think of the small space occupied by a church notice, which possibly costs a guinea or two, and the large area occupied by an article by the clergyman of the same church it is not difficult to imagine the almost overwhelming effect of the article in filling his church.

How to obtain this publicity is certainly no easy matter. But this much can be said with confidence —a great deal of work is required to get any publicity and more than work, a great deal of thought. Before launching a publicity campaign one must think out all the unusual angles which can possibly be envisaged, bearing in mind that papers like unusual and interesting information. For example, the clergyman who holes out in one on the local golf course is much more likely to obtain publicity by sending in this information than if he merely sent in information that he had finished a round "three up and two to go". In brief then that is the secret of getting this free publicity —send in suitable material with real interest value and where possible keep it brief.

One manner of obtaining free publicity which many people do not use is to send photographs. As a rule pictures have far more pulling power than words. A suitable caption can always be added, for instance, "Mrs. William Smith landing a 3lb. trout. Mrs. Smith is the wife of the author of *River Fly Fishing*." A paper might readily publish a photograph of the author's wife when it would decline one of the author himself. Publicity is of course thus obtained for the book and the people whom such a picture would attract are the very people who might buy it.

16

Resignations, Applications for Membership, Semi-Official Letters, Appeals, etc.

THE most important thing to say about resignations is that they are often accepted, therefore do not resign from something in a fit of temper if you do not really want to. A letter of resignation is quite a simple thing and can be written in some such form as the undernoted examples.

(a) As I am leaving the district I wish to tender my resignation as a member of the Farmers' Association Executive Committee. May I take this opportunity of saying that I have enjoyed being a member of this committee and shall be very sorry to lose the friendship and companionship it has afforded.

(b) I wish to tender my resignation as chairman of the Downs Cricket Club. I am very sorry to have to do this, but my doctor has advised me that my cricket days are over.

Application for Membership

I write to inquire if I may become a member of the Brayside Tennis Club. I think I can claim that my standard of play is about average as I was a member of the Calverley Club for three years, but have just moved into this district. If my application is acceptable I shall be pleased to hear from you with particulars.

Letters to Officials

With so many nationalized services occasions may arise when letters have to be written to officials. In the ordinary way this type of correspondence can be treated just as any other social or business affair, but trouble frequently arises in the time taken to receive a reply. One has to realize the mentality and also the difficulty of the Government officer in his task. Unlike all ordinary business men he is frequently not allowed to give a decision; alternatively, his decision cannot be given until some decision has been made higher up the line. This naturally can cause a great deal of delay to the member of the public. It is not usually very much use trying to fight a Government official in the normal way because you, as an individual, have very little power whereas the Government has immense power and of course, thanks to the tax-payer, immense wealth. Nevertheless, there is a technique which may be employed.

I think the methods most likely to succeed in dealing with Government departments and officials can be listed in the following order of importance:

(i)   Patience;
(ii) Persistence;
(iii) Courage;
(iv) Very polite suggestions, which might almost be called threats of exposure in some way if something is not done. But care to avoid any personal blackmail is required.

To deal with these points one by one. Patience is necessary because of the interminable delay which sometimes occurs. Persistence is essential because part of the reason for the delaying tactics is possibly the hope that you will become tired and abandon your correspondence. Keep on writing and referring to previous letters and the fact that you have still not had a satisfactory reply and so on, in other words try to wear out the Government official rather than let him tire you. You must have the courage of your convictions and not allow any official to frighten you or try to intimidate you— you must fight on all fronts if you would obtain your needs.

The last heading is the most important and the most helpful of all in trying to achieve anything with a Government department. Such "threats" are not libellous threats in the sense that you are libelling any individual. Nevertheless, they form one of the main hopes of getting anything done. You have several lines of approach; if there is one, you can suggest that you will take the matter to a higher authority; alternatively, you can threaten to use the right of every subject to have the matter raised by your Member of Parliament. Unfortunately, Members of Parliament are usually very busy and quite often this threat is less effective than it should be. Again, press publicity is something which all Government departments and Government officials are apt to fear, especially if they are in the wrong. A gentle hint that you may be able to have the matter put in the press may bring surprising results.

There are, of course, a number of other methods which can be employed in the face of difficulties with a Government department, but these are outside the scope of this book and would require expert legal advice and guidance. The main thing to remember is this inherent fear of their superiors or publicity from which most civil servants suffer and it is a very real one indeed. Provided you keep within the law and are within your rights by playing on this fear favourable results may often be obtained. Where interviews can be arranged they are usually better than letters. Another great secret is always to avoid losing your temper although pretending to be furious is often an excellent tactic.

17

Forms of Address and Subscription

FORTUNATELY, there is less formality in addressing people of different rank nowadays than there was of old, and much less importance is attached to any minor slip.

I give below a list which I have extracted from my other book, *Business Letters, Contracts and Etiquette*. (Paperfront companion volume.)

PERSONS OF RANK*

A list of forms of address for persons of rank is given in *Chambers's Dictionary*, but I give below some of the more common ranks, with examples:

DUKE	His Grace the Duke of	My Lord Duke or your Grace (refer to as "Your Grace"). (I remain, my Lord Duke).
DUCHESS	Her Grace the Duchess of	Madam (refer to as "Your Grace"). I remain, Madam).
MARQUESS	The Most Hon. the Marquis of	My Lord Marquis (refer to as "Your Lordship"). (I remain, My Lord Marquis).

*Some use has been made of *Chambers's Dictionary*, by kind permission of the publishers, Messrs. W. & R. Chambers, Ltd.

MARCHIONESS	The Most Hon. the Marchioness of	Madam (refer to as "Your Ladyship"). I remain, Madam).
EARL	The Right Hon. the Earl of	My Lord (refer to as "Your Lordship"). I remain, My Lord).
COUNTESS	The Right Hon. the Countess of	Madam (refer to as "Your Ladyship"). (I remain, Madam).
VISCOUNT	The Right Hon. the (Lord) Viscount	My Lord (refer to as "Your Lordship"). (I remain, My Lord).
VISCOUNTESS	The Right Hon. the Viscountess, or The Viscountess	Madam (refer to as "Your Ladyship"). (I remain, Madam).
BARON	The Right Hon. Lord or, The Lord	My Lord ("Your Lordship"). (I remain, My Lord).
BARONESS	*Chambers:* The Right Hon. the, or, The Baroness	My Lady ("Your Ladyship"). (I remain, My Lady).
BARONET	Sir James Milwall, Bart., or Bt.	Sir (I am, Sir).
BARONET'S WIFE	Lady Milwall	Madam ("Your Ladyship"). (I am, Madam).
KNIGHT	Sir John Newell	Sir (between friends, Dear Sir John). (I am, Sir).
KNIGHT'S WIFE	Lady Newell	Madam (between friends, Dear Lady —). (I am, Madam).
ARCHBISHOP (English)	His Grace the Lord Archbishop of	My Lord Archbishop (Your Grace).

BISHOP	The Right Rev. the Lord Bishop of, or The Lord Bishop of	My Lord Bishop (Your Lordship).
DEAN	The Very Rev. the Dean of	Very Rev. Sir (formal). Mr. Dean.
CLERGY	The Rev. William Lockwood. (If a Doctor of Divinity, add D.D.).	Rev. Sir (formal). Dear Sir, Dear Mr., or, if a D.D., Dear Dr.
JUDGE	The Hon. Mr. Justice	Sir.
PRIVY COUNCILLORS	The Right Hon. Michael Quartley, M.P.	Sir. (Yours faithfully).
MEMBERS OF PARLIAMENT	David Jones, Esq., M.P. Sir Roy Farjeon, M.P.	Sir. (Yours faithfully). or Dear Sir.
DOCTOR OR SURGEON	Dr. Peter Ransome or more politely, Peter Ransome, Esq., M.D. (A surgeon is always addressed Philip Palmer, Esq., F.R.C.S., M.D., etc., and called Mr. not Doctor.)	Dear Sir or Dear Doctor. A surgeon, Dear Sir, or Dear Mr.

Any degrees used, e.g. B.A., B.Sc., are put after the Esq., Thus: J. Smith, Esq., B.A.

Commissioned Officers of H.M. Forces are addressed by rank, together with decorations, if any. Naval Officers, add R.N., Army Officers may have their arm of Service added, e.g. R.A., R.E.

Persons of ordinary rank.

TWO OR MORE MARRIED WOMEN	Mesdames
TWO OR MORE SPINSTERS	The Misses
HUSBAND AND WIFE	Mr. and Mrs. (No initials of degrees, etc.)
BOYS UNDER 14	Master

ONE LADY	Dear Madam
Two business women can be addressed simply in the head of the letter as:	Ladies
PROFESSIONAL MAN, BUSINESS MAN	Dear Sir
OR TRADESMAN	(Esq., on Envelope)
MANUAL WORKER (Usually)	Mr. (Mr. on Envelope)

A BUSINESS FIRM: Messrs. J. BLANK & Co., Ltd.
(The short for Messrs. is M/S.)

Index

Car Driving in 2 Weeks

and Hints for all motorists.

by **L. Nathan (R.A.C. Diploma)**

A whole course in one astounding book –
26th revised edition – over one million sold!

**What the Critics say:

Daily Telegraph – 'Immensely practical'
Daily Sketch – 'Excellent for new motorists'
The Motor – 'A book worth having'
The Autocar – 'No learner could fail to benefit'
Birmingham Post – 'Certainly the *best*'
Edinburgh Evening News – 'A notable contribution'
Highland News – 'A bible for "L" Drivers'

UNIFORM WITH THIS BOOK

ELLIOT RIGHT WAY BOOKS

Kingswood, Surrey, U.K.

OUR PUBLISHING POLICY

HOW WE CHOOSE

Our policy is to consider every deserving manuscript and we can give special editorial help where an author is an authority on his subject but an inexperienced writer. We are rigorously selective in the choice of books we publish. We set the highest standards of editorial quality and accuracy. This means that a *Paperfront* is easy to understand and delightful to read. Where illustrations are necessary to convey points of detail, these are drawn up by a subject specialist artist from our panel.

HOW WE KEEP PRICES LOW

We aim for the big seller. This enables us to order enormous print runs and achieve the lowest price for you. Unfortunately, this means that you will not find in the *Paperfront* list any titles on obscure subjects of minority interest only. These could not be printed in large enough quantities to be sold for the low price at which we offer this series.

We sell almost all our *Paperfronts* at the same unit price. This saves a lot of fiddling about in our clerical departments and helps us to give you world-beating value. Under this system, the longer titles are offered at a price which we believe to be unmatched by any publisher in the world.

OUR DISTRIBUTION SYSTEM

Because of the competitive price, and the rapid turnover, *Paperfronts* are possibly the most profitable line a bookseller can handle. They are stocked by the best bookshops all over the world. It may be that your bookseller has run out of stock of a particular title. If so, he can order more from us at any time—we have a fine reputation for "same day" despatch, and we supply any order, however small (even a single copy), to any bookseller who has an account with us. We prefer you to buy from your bookseller, as this reminds him of the strong underlying public demand for *Paperfronts*. Members of the public who live in remote places, or who are housebound, or whose local bookseller is unco-operative, can order direct from us by post.

FREE

If you would like an up-to-date list of all the paperfront titles currently available, send a stamped self-addressed envelope to
ELLIOT RIGHT WAY BOOKS, BRIGHTON RD.,
LOWER KINGSWOOD, SURREY, U.K.